DESIRE LINES

Jessica Mookherjee is the author of three pamphlets and three full collections of poetry. Tigress (Nine Arches Press) was shortlisted for best second collection in the Ledbury Munthe Prize. She has had poems highly commended in the Forward Prize twice (in 2017 & 2021). She is co-editor of Against the Grain Press.

Also by Jessica Mookherjee

Notes from a Shipwreck	(Nine Arches Press, 2022)
Play Lists	(Broken Sleep Books, 2021)
Tigress	(Nine Arches Press, 2019)
Flood	(Cultured Llama, 2018)
Joyride	(Black Light Engine Room, 2017)
The Swell	(Telltale Press, 2016)

Desire Lines

Jessica Mookherjee

ISBN: 978-1-915079-91-6

The author has asserted their right to be identified as the author of this Work in accordance with the Copyright, Designs and Patents Act 1988

Cover designed by Aaron Kent

Edited & Typeset by Aaron Kent

Broken Sleep Books Ltd
Rhydwen
Talgarreg
Ceredigion
SA44 4HB

Broken Sleep Books Ltd
Fair View
St Georges Road
Cornwall
PL26 7YH

Contents

For All The People I lived with in London

Tyburn Blossom

Shimmer and Flicker, slick cab driver quicks her
round the corner, laughs off the fare, says
don't you get smart green girl– like the hicks from the sticks
who in no time, think London's not so clever clever.

Fast lights, torch eyes. Can't hold on to her hat which flies with a
gust from the tube into Baker Street Station. *Watch your bag, green
girl, watch your back.* Walk with that carpet bag across concrete.
Something big and hemmed in takes her hand, says *turn around, take
it all in.* Montpellier Rise, Brent Cross, climb the overpass to the big
Sainsbury's, buy fruit she's never seen to wean on and sink in a duck
egg cot with kids from places with exotic names; *East Grinstead,
Hassocks, Potters Bar.* They write *Keep Out* on the fridge door. Puss
in Boots on the night bus, where a bloke called Mo says she's too
much in the wrong place. Out with boy from Belsize Park under big
sky, leather jacket smart in his high ceiling one room bedsit another
shade of brick, stucco and lights, where they're hair-sprayed and
dyed. After the *Bad Seeds* at Brixton's Fridge, a suckle in the local
café. He asks her to run away with him if she'll switch for the rent,
to SW9   *strangler, street-pad, cut-*
                                                            purse.

He gets her a foetus, *look after it for me,* he says and disappears. Many
men knocking, blue lights, black stockings, blood spatter outside the
Swan. On that old morning, make up caked into carpets, baby gone,
she runs.

Marie picks her up in her red car after she got paid for the bit part
at the BBC, they go up West One, huddle under dental drills and
the fire escape in Wimpole Street, frolic in panic rooms and down
big staircases, nick light-bulbs from John Lewis, take cabs but never
pay. Teenager-cool drinking vodka lime in club toilets with a goth

called Damage Control. The moon's still, reminds her of flowers, while she busies with pretty eyes and stolen cheque books, zips up a no-good heart that knows it's somewhere under the books she stole. She carries cardboard boxes full of toys, prams, powdered milk, Bonjella and spliff. Excitable-numb, sucks thumb, grows hair in W1 with all her fingers and in a box room in W11, the smell of sinsemilla in the air, an ever-summer above a shop called *Bizarre Bazar*, ferments in the Golden Hinds and the Crown, punch drunk on Benylin and acid, piles her mates in, plays séance on a glass hot line, asks *Is there anybody there?* John Lennon answers, says to give him some peace in heaven and they scream and laugh. She sorts her vinyl collection, smokes with boys, blags a job in the Record and Tape exchange, spend nights piling up fried chicken boxes, coca cola cans.

They'll catch you, urchin, doxy. Cut-purse, foot-pad, felon, they'll never catch you alive, on the run.

Risk Ways

Filch the filth in N7, derelict Irishman, bottles of Guinness, seventies carpets. Hides out there at the World's End, at the Nag's Head. New light morning, dirt like nothing ever seen before, smell of stale tobacco falling into pub floors. She nicks bottles of Martini, incense, a black and white TV, a book on Lou Reed with a stolen credit card. Card sharp. Be local, has a joke with the veterans propping up the bar, walls become glass. She's huckster with her slick back hair gel and mod tucker, practise spells, spelling and magic tricks, bit-faker blabbing for a break, all hokum-cokum and cold coffee left out all night, with roaches and Marlborough Lights.

Milch cow for the babes, passed the guesthouse, banged up by the bill, who see through her, green girl, back of the cell. Wait to see what the beaks have on her. *Don't tell, don't tell*. The darkmans of it all, the hopeless Indian moll, see her going home. The pigeons are darker then she'd ever pocket, nicks a quid to avoid a lagging, screws eyes to nubs stubbed out on the rub.

They call her *lucky girl* and *off her rocker*. Her mistake, nothing means more then the moon as she scours the streets for a snakesman, a sauce-box, a girl in a ghetto in a pack and a pickle, all off her chump. Disappears down those roads, Jackson Road, Holloway Road, Hornsey Road, Lowman Road. The newsagent shouts to her in Bengali as she runs down the mud sunken A1 to the Enkil Arms. They know her face, her caste, made the news again today. Hide out there for some time. Archway dirt stares and debris melts her down, housing office, Medina Road, Harvest Estate and Sobell sports centre red paint. Runs risk road to the Seven Sisters, where she lies low in N15 for a month till the devil blows over. High on speed to stay awake, pretends to like Arsenal, pretends to hate East Ham, waits for hook and hoist, to watch a clock, Glock and half morning until the rent's paid. A man follows in a car as she walks down the middle of the road at night, says *get in*. She stares into his eyes asks him what kind of man he is, grins him down with the knife in her smile as he drives away.

Grove

Tears away at dead time when eyes bright with lack less and dew,
devil girl, Devi, purse in her hand, goes night walking,
stray down Blackstock Road in pointed shoes with worn sole,
don't tell anyone where you've gone. The wrong side,
meander river-like towards Plimsoll Road, Monsell Road,
Wilberforce Road, something catches her eye-glint into a space
she can't know, all things ahead to catch her, the luck of the draw.

Tear-away, Toe-rag, a cut in the side of your purse girl, go
wandering down old greenways, green lanes until she hits
herself in the face with a honey shaw, frock and frox
in an iron gate dell marked on the side of Drayton Park.
She sees the nastyman off in the dark roads and wisp
becomes an eye, becomes a tail, and the gap in the gate
where it lets you in. *Here, there's a croaker singing for you,*

come in pollywog, buttercup, frog's foot, rain girl, sit in the land
where it gives way, tell the whole of North London who's come
this way and who'll she'll bring here again in the spring.
Who will do your Damage? Who will be the pie-man? Madcap boys
with moon faces dark, they won't know that's the sharp
of it, won't admit to what she found. This clearing, unbuilt
ground in a pop of spawn egg land, lunder, London's moon path.

Red Paths

Simmering in N4, scores a crooked mile and walks the bridge to the park at night. Speaks to trees near the railway lines, walks red paths, Green Lanes, holy ways, hiss back at men, thumps the tops of cars, always dawn light, cherry blossom, boundary stones and lost keys.   *Know your place cut-purse girl.*
Watch your back.

A dark old rumour sits with her in Eel Pie House and the Tavern, throws rocks into the boarded river and she wants to hold a revolver, bury lungs in the marsh, walk across brushwood into the tip of the Island, hears buskers caves into concrete. She's made of brick and sand dust, walks past the dolly-shops to Essex Road. Down N1, down and draws a long-bow into time's desire line. It's there, where she is, near the fag and mag shops, where she's a lonely flash and flying mess until something says

Turn around, take it all in   be the ghost of this place

She walk down paths, waves twenty years through time to the spot where she turns around, picks up what's left of the gold, at the Whittington, cut to size, the damage gets done, cauterized   *Cut purse girl, foot pad,   watch your back, hold your own with the boys.*   The Dried Flower shop, The Stuffed Animal shop, The Record and Tape
shop, blood sun sets on Islington Green and cutlass smart on the 73, blags her way into Gower Street and they won't deliver Pizza to the Marquis Estate.

Cut Purse   Toe-Rag,   Turn again.

Blind Alleys

There, there nipper, steels the key from her old lady's kipper. No fungus on his face, good clobber keeps her looking, offers her molly, knows she could do better. There was all that bad business down the railway lines, she remembers, those tricks, but it serves her to stitch it together, some good tunes in her record collection, some tall tales to keep him keen, drugs and cards. She gets coke and chips and he orders beer. She says it smells of disinfectant in here and he holds her hand. Thanks her for that night where she put up with him, says he still owes her speed and acid and a bottle of gin. He tells her, in the burger bar on Holloway Road, the Soloman Grundy, the Queen's Head, the Nags Head, he tells her because there is nothing else to tell. There he is with a two bob job, blown like a bottle with his zhushed up hair. His tells are queer, how his fam disappeared down blind alleys and dead ends. It's best not to know how the story ends, best to keep the secrets but he keeps on, spills his drink all over her dress.

Hollow Ways

She takes her cards out, one by one, takes after her poor old duck,
who lies in bed all day with a bad back, dosed up on tamoxifen, a
looker in her day. The old man turns cards around, *here's the burn-
card*, all the way round, card-sharp. She's here now, in the sunken
roads, somewhere to go, somewhere to be found. She sees it in there
as the chips are down, That back of the cab job, will it come out that
she's sunken and dipped. Was it that old man playing knick knack?
She knows the answer but can't tell. Slight of hand girl, nymph of
the discard tray, gives it the patter. Says it doesn't matter, gets into
cars with strangers, beards and taxi drivers. *Turned out again.* Pitter-
patter down the Holloway, in ruby slippers for the pocket-trick.
Keeps you looking at the kiss-me-quick while the mark misses the
trick. She goes box-jumping down Finsbury Park all the while the
true odds stay down. She can't stay schtum, chitter chatter, don't give
the game away. Zigzag girl bends her back down the Hollow Ways.

Trench

Dora always get's her man. *Don't give me that Jolene crap*, she says and slaps and drags. *Give me back*. While you were filching down Finsbury Park, while you were out with the follow-me-lads, while you were out the cat's about. It's war-painted and tainted now. Where do you go all day, chitter? We watch you out of the windows, where do you go to see him? Zeus-Pitterpatter, or someone better? Where do you get the dosh, wind-sucker? Either way, here's curses hurled at you. You'll be a fag ash girl for the honey-polony, with your manky mincing and mollying – you'll never call this home, you'll be the never-be-loved. Dora's lost her rag, unpretty rage and racket, must be the fairest in this this trench of land that passes through the woods and droves. She thinks she's been such a good girl to get that rough trade home.

Sunken Lanes

She turns into moon-girl, the mirror girl all lipstick and drag, an ashtray girl. Chain-smoking down the ladder where the boys call to her in a language she half remembers, say they'll see her alright if she calls round the back. They call her *sister*. She's beside the water the night the deer calls her, they can't see her so she gets louder. She's beside the ponds when the vixen calls her. Every night she waits for Jack in the Green, every night she hopes he'll wake her there. She's no body, there's no body there. She can't see herself in the hall mirror. They live in a juggler's box, one room by a tree across from the park. Jack's a snakesman with magic words all for himself, blind oaths and charms. She; on her ghost walks mutters *abracadabra* and *sim-sala-bim* to no effect. Jack's the juggler after a hat production, wants a zig-zag girl to tear him to pieces, but everyone hides the mirrors, don't show him what he could be. *How do I Look?* Jack asks her, in his natty threads.

Bubble up from the old river, fleet foot, dam the river, curse the ground, that's where she's found most days now, smokes spliff and throws darts. Here in the hunting grounds. Here at the sagg ponds, the Eden point of London's two sunken rivers, its dens and kens. She's forest-watched, each step she takes by the water edge, merges with drinking leaves. She pops the head in her mouth, *bottom's up, the game's up*, Queen Mab will see you now. *Clap clap*, the weather turns, the old queen, her gaping flaps, *they keep you, secret you*, nymph about behind your back, never tell you how sweet you smell.

Flower girl,   numb girl,   *see what you can become.*

River flows into those children, all were girls once, *girl girl, knave girl*, at the brook Jack turns dark water, a taste of sewer on his mouth, going underground by being stopped. *I can't hold you any longer*, an old man cries, *I'm broken in two with my own hands.* But these are his hands. The lines on her palms cross in tributaries and deltas, make a map of the tube lines and tunnels for to follow. She sees with her eye-water lit up by the sun, London's lights from Primrose Hill climbs into her smile. Ivy stretches into her toes, holds in the binding of each step before she drinks from the water. She sees how beautiful she is as a tree shines in fast light, how it catches the dust, how it sprinkles breath in a ripple of scent, she sees for the first time, how beautiful she is. The green of London's secret paths.

Causeway

Where does she go? Up to no good kid. She is blood mouth trailing scent. She knows where the lights dim, all the wells spring as she runs step by step, Clerkenwell, Baggnigge Well, Bridewell, Holy well, Clement's well, Sadler's Wells. Tips her lips, drinks from each, one by one. Catch herself as she runs, all well. She's runnels, ripples and her pebbles bright with urge to see her live. She's no body, she's nobody, can't feel anything but urgency, a gust of breath that sings and slams onto concrete buildings, searches for the frequency to find a green boy. Disappears down Ealde Street, down Hochestone, the catch on the breeze to look. Is he calling her on the wind, juggler Jack, Occus bochus, Loki, *that* bloke? She can only hear a voice in her head, no heart open only rising air and a swarm of mist. Did she forget this? Jack'll be where they once walked, up that hill, all vinegar pasted, where he once tasted her. She stops. Just where the river rises, is that him, covered in leaves? She knew she'd find him, knows how he's fixed, whistles, full of moxie, on his ear and neck.

Strand

She turns into the pool, stops her mouth of songs. She drinks from the flowers that grow where she stands, calls to the sky, to the earth, the green to take her. She can't go home looking like that, all dripping and black. Dressed in McQueen, London watches her back, walks up to the crying girl; out of a fashion magazine, garlanded, tartan and blood. Calls her name out from the cloud burst end of storm, gust-smack left in the roadside kill, says, *Branwen, Bridgid, Morigan,* what happens to love when it doesn't come back? Are you listening? The city girl takes out a pack of John Players, opens a bag of crisps, sips from her lips, rips a hole in her chest and stubs out her cigarette, a road, a path, a lane, a sithe and serpentine. The city blows smoke from her fag, *and in the mirror of you, girl the mirror of you, girl. Oh poor cow, you think you've got the guts to leave your stitches alone now?* The city laughs, big throat choke fun. Louder then the wind louder then the wind louder then the wind louder. *Grow up. I'll turn you hoofer, prancer, get in with the chancers and shush all the dish you can eat, girlfriend. We'll go up town again and score. Take that song you sing and sing it more, louder then the wind till the raven's return to Primrose Hill.*

Depositary

Signals and red dust musters, the tinker takes
her under. Bury the waste in the depositary,
near the milk column, near the used johnnies
and the rubber dummies. She never looks back,
shuts her mouth. Coram Fields, where the clever
girls tear their skirts to give them hope. She's blood
soaked and medieval. The rain runs through her,
sieves her bones. *Leave it alone.* Perhaps it'll return
with another man's face. There's a lot riding
on a bottle of gin and a hat pin, *goose girl, golden eggs.*
Scam the bolt shut before it gets through the gate. Go
down the pub with the whip-jacks, show them how
its done. Keep your chin up to the bones... *and those little
bones.* All washed up in the tidal melt, a flash of yellow tin.

Soft Estate

Scrubbed and floored, she walks past Canonbury, never looks back
at those pie-men, those follow-me-lads. Give the glad-eye with
her fairy-boots, ready for action comic book sighs. *This'll do*, looks
round the box room in N16, She's still a few marks and tricks up
her sleeve. It's the same old Jackanory.

Keep walking   Don't look back   Keys in your hand.

Safe in the cemetery, Abney Park busy, unconsecrated, counts
up pennies for bus fare for a job summoning devils, makes up
her CV, walks the streets of Camden, Kentish Town,
Kings Cross. Likes her madmen Hawksmoor smart but puts up
with the art school Hoxton lads if they'll buy her a drink
on a Saturday night. Church Street café's selling aubergines,
vegetarian Indian food, vegan pubs play punk rock, Victorian Grove
squatters meet in her bedroom, watch filth beat people up. The man
downstairs calls night-watch at 3am, she slops out in Dalston drug
dens with speed dealers and men wearing lipstick, wigs and tights
and she's all magic carpets, hummus and camel lights, bumps into
the past by the Cock Tavern, hides in alleyways to avoid them

*Don't I know you? Cut-purse girl, highway robber, foot-pad. Exorcist, Charlatan
Soothe-sayer, card-sharp,   trick or treat?*

In The Jolly Butchers they queue to woo her, lipstick, pencil-lead,
gin-sheen sky over Clissold Park, in north sixteen, she's postcodes,
made-up codes, fizz in bottles, still walking, learning lines, having
cappuccino, pasta and jazz on Saturday night, the city winks.

Flinted, livlied up in second-hand Chanel and fake pearls, sits in
Hilmarten Road to be one of the girls, they drink cheep wine, talk
about men they knew, pinch of salt, hand grenades, sexual assault,

coffee and cake in NW1. Betty and Vasilis run off to Thailand without her, leave her dry. So she taps Marie from Rowley Way, who's moved to a tower block since her hair fell out, shows her all those old LP's and newspaper clips from her John Peel days, she's been on TV and everything, faded pop star.

Beaten Track

She's a smash and grab, stand backstage in the George Robey with the rest of the band, play bad tunes, bad times, holds onto the man in the Garage who's name she never asks. Walks down flickering lit roads at night, follows trails of stones, starts to know what the City's made of her, lays down lines of crumbs, listens out for the tub-thump of brass and drum as pied piper comes, he says *follow me, follow the bread and rock, follow me to the chaunting lay chavvy, the kiss me quick bars.*

Be the top of the class, jump crab shells, eat jellied eels, listen to siren swell and bus doors open, mind the gap and evening standard. She's jam packed with cupboard love, walks and walking. Lays on Hampstead Heath in long grass, sees the city from Primrose Hill, dives into the wind, becomes an eclipse that stops the world's path around the sun. Think the boys blind. When she's got her scrolls and cash, written letters to all and sundry, Marie tells her in certain terms, she'll meet no one just sitting there all day, makes her dinner parties, invites minor celebrities once seen on TV, comedians and some old has-been rock star who says she's the dial-burst, fire wiring and flash. But she's beaten tracks, and the grass of the city grows through her, pavements get under fingers, she scratches, pinches dreams from discount paperbacks and vending machines. Marie takes her in a white Triumph Spitfire to see the witch in Archway. *I'll sit outside to make sure you see her, get that glamour out of you so you can see better.* In N19 Marie grins supermodel lips and crosses her long limbs on the dash, watches as the green girl goes in *you'll learn to be me*

cut purse girl,   *footpad.*

Greenway

The city shrinks inside her, turns tricks of guilt and amber kisses,
men at kerbsides, kebab shops, pound shops, bury them in the forest
shops, cop shops. Hustling, she knows it. There's no point to it, she
says, pointing to it, to park land, sea shore, cliff edge. She could paint
in aggregate, build love in gravel dipped in calcium, shells and blast
furnace, slag and iron ore.   *Turn again, turn heads again*

Choke Point

Hung out in a paradise left to day-fade, where canal joins slum
and cemetery, where a house is left to defy and a park is verb
and botany, she wants to be found but no one comes. She lights
matches at dark, smoke and summons the dead from headphones,
becomes vigilante, knight of the brush, a dash of something, kill-
calf and slinger. She's agony-piler, bottleneck and tag. *Toe-rag*, right
it, *write it down*, steal for the long-debt, and spinner, spin it
like an arch dell, turn grass into gold, gives them the name of her
first born, *kiss the toad*.

SkyLarker

Full of Micky Bliss and Tom Tit, Betty gets back with Vasilis,
he shacks back in Holloway, kicks off to kopse the cornflakes
on Lorraine Road, she moans it's all Greek to her and he won't
commit though the sex is good, so she gets a new flat mate near the
reservoirs. Skint, even though they tell things can only get better.
Brit-popped and cidered in the Good Mixer, and *time-to-fly Angel*.

The rent-rising and she's skylark turned magpie, wants all her hair-
clips and shiny things. Marie says *don't go back green girl, keep step
with the times*. So she goes to the Dogs, the roundabout rough land
ready for big sky and swing of air, they say things are better now at
the East End, E15, need the 69 from Walthamstow
to get home, it rains and the market's full of plastic, they look at
each other and complain. *I'm all better now*, she says to Marie, gets
some plants, a magic carpet and a gangster landlord counting cash
in the kitchen. She goes to the forest where people disappear.

Flight Paths

She hides out, upstairs from Sharon, who's brother was killed in a
pub fight, smashed with a snooker cue and her daughter looks like
Hitler, but spitting and tatoo'd, and Sharon yells *why can't you be
like her, get an education, a job,* She looks at the girl and mouths *cut
purse girl, foot pad, felon, come with me to E17, babysitter, throat slitter.*

Downstairs from the peeping tom who trains his telescope to look
into Lorraine's bathroom and her daughter, Siobhan hides in her
flat, plays chess and says, *teach me that gospel shark, beak, all learner
shover, teach me how to be a water caster, we've got no books no plants
or wallpaper, just floorboards and a big TV from Asda* and green girl
whispers:

come with me to the forest and I'll show you seedling, sapling,
sapwood, crown, show you what you can become. *Take her, take her
pied piper, take the city rats and shaker makers.* Dressed in pied and
motley, covers mottle and daub on the city lines, follow pigeons and
magpies into the woods, finds the witches house, tell your secrets to
limber your timbers, *cut purse, foot pad, felon,*

tricheor, beak bunting   out of the never never where the
Marxists died. They go to the dogs on a Saturday night, watch
them chase hares on the back of her neck, makes noise, hides in
quarries, hangs out with William Morris in Epping Forest. The
birds show her the best places, dirty spaces, found wrapped on the
roundabouts and the old estates where she's flown.

Lovers Lanes

Silver Street, N18, above a pram shop, she sees him in the light of glow worms and pumpkin carriages, say *I do* to a gown and bike chain. He kisses her by the traffic lights on Fore Street and she doesn't think

he's who he says he is, can see the moss in his hair, the sea in his eyes, they hot-foot to the Hackney Downs, in E5, makes her Tai food, she asks him what music he likes. He only likes rap and sea shanties, and he doesn't know much about the bands

she likes, just knows what tastes good, takes hash from her mouth with his long spoon and they follow crumbs home. The moon's big the night of Lady Di's crash and he cries that morning when the blue boy says he loves her back.

Bridle Way

St. James Street, E17, borrow a mattress, scrub and rub it. Swaps guitars for sitars and the dhol drums. He tries to set the place alight. They walk the longest tat market in search of Tupperware and Basmati rice.

I'm not your absinthe mother, I'm not your absent mother.

He cooks her Sunday dinner after Sunday dinner. *See what we've become,* he says, puts a computer on the landing, play house on the fire escape, as the city heat sails and they watch stars turn into helicopters and chem-trails. A Bomber's jacked all the yuppie places, racists, anti-gays, anti-blacks; he missed them in the Banglatown mela, but got the pavement cafes. She can't afford a sofa in Habitat. Walk Old Compton Street, circle the Angel in search of merry-men, meets the follow-me-lad as Jarvis predicted, at the millennium and she laughs at how he tries to impress her.

Let's all meet up in the year two thousand, all fully grown...

His art shown in a glass house, every thing transparent, she can see right through him, everything new, everything better, he's all better now he lies, hands out pictures of his boy-face and his date of birth to passers by.

Roll-up, come see the follow-me-lad face the nubbing-cheat, get his pickers broken

and he hands the flyers out at Angel Station, where punters bin them and papers fly litter and skitter into the New River. Streets are cleaned on time, the trains shine on time and they hang out at the Saatchi, admire pictures of Myra Hindly, all the people come and go talking of Tracy Emin. From the Imax to the BFI, the embankment

and OXO tower, the Barbican and Lumier, eat in good restaurants
and couple up on the top of the Bus and she gets a job selling water
and air to the thirsty and choked. Between SE18 and SE1, Lambeth
Walk and the Cut and shove, the Woolwich Ferry. *Take it all in*
Thrust and push, mobile phone mush and look back in the river
to the frozen girl,

whirl again matchstick girl, warm yourself, warn. The worn ways
of the cut purse girl,   watch your back   watch
yourself.

Mudlark

The 68 to the mudflats, lorry unload at the slime strip-line,
shine on waterlap, greentide, walks onto a roar and churn,
mudlark, sunburn and berry-red at sea gull beaked chops,
with pocket-money for chips, across the Thames, back and wash,
the foot tunnel, green spiral

make a wish, urchin, cut-purse, foot-pad, mud-lark, sea-sick, winkle-picker,
spikenard. Time to cross the river, watch your feet, cut glass, pig-girl.

dip salt river into cranes. Royal Arsenal, rose tattoo, henbane.
Meet Aslan from the wardrobe in the park loos and into the old
bank where the mums gather for housing advice, smoke dodgy fags.

She's buzzed in on the eighteenth floor, SE18, Tanya's got two kids,
at seventeen, she's not been well, her mum's her backbone,
sister's her right arm, she knows who killed that black kid
in Eltham. The man from Somalia a few doors down tells green girl
he spent his rent on doing up his car, its how he earns and burns,

bought an electric guitar. It makes sense as he rolls up
next to the whale road. She mudslings back across the river
to E11 and the Baker's Arms, past mudspit where they build
the Millennium's home. As mud becomes tower and dome
she stands under an avenue of clocks and shopping malls,

glamour, nail clipped grass in decoturf, kept smart
by private security guards, and the filthy foam of the grey dirt
swan's way tapping the tide line up and down the world's edge,
cutpurse, limehouse, water sharp and break. Marie holds her hand,
rests it on her belly. *It's time to sell fruit and pram into the future,*

*girl, it's time to ring out your bells now there's money in your lucy-locket
and fish to batter your thighs with. Come on, girl, it's time and high
tide.*

Old Straight Track

Watch your step. The Millenium bug makes her morning sick,
looks down river, walks passed the shopping centre
on Lewisham High Street, pass Fitness First and high blood
pressure, pass Mothercare and Catford Gun Shop,
the twenty foot cat that appears, hugs the arcade.
Watch your step, duck the dive to stay alive, lamb
to slaughter, post-partum, can he carry you? Say's he'll marry
you, mog and sprog, keep you ripper and nipper
down Whitechapel and Bethnal Green, down the shine
of the Jubilee Line. Can you afford the house on Windmill Lane
where old Rome falls and chokes in his claret? Is it time?
Is his strong arm enough for you to mix with? Can he fix this?
Watch your step. Nip a purse for the bowsing ken, the derelict
ground, the crack den, jack-pot and Railway Tavern,
is this what she'll fuse with? Keep cement mixer churn
from the Forrester's Arms to the working men's club from setting
hard inside her. He says he'll make money, build a helicopter
landing pad and an Olympic Stadium inside her.

Ditch

Stray Battersea cat, hides in the boompoint of a crane,
that winks and lets her down by red light, *come down rat catcher,*
on your Jack Jones for some how's your father, a bit of the glimmer
to use your loaf to get a bun in the oven baked and stoked, peddle
where the cows would pass to slaughter, old abattoir, martyr
marker where the Russian men piss their cigarette ends
arcing over front gardens. Sheila comes round to talk about the bins,
her husband's back problems, been on the sick for twenty years.
They've all moved out, the Culpeppers, Chadwicks, Buckleys and Frys.

Sold up, gone to Redbridge as the house prices rise. The filchmen
knock Angel cottage down, oldest house in the East End, survived
the Blitz, it won't win a medal in the next Olympics. The gypsy
horses move through Angel Lane, Cobham Road, Wickham Way.
The shop next door with a sticky floor keeps a gun, sells chewing
gum, cheep cider and nothing else. Maryland is rain, sex shops,
scaffolding, a cafe that serves peirogi and strong beer. Sheila thinks
they should stay round here and get Amerjit to take those brown
tiles off the bathroom walls, he'll do it cheep, strip the woodchip,
swears by the lightmans he'll do the job, won't budge a beak, *watch
your back, he'll have your gigger's jacked, tattle and tic, cut purse, home
breaker, rat catcher.*

All night she hears the man from Ghana, three doors down,
coughing asbestos lung, thug of boot on gut. Calls the police,
I think he's dead outside my house. *Attractive two bedroom,
newly refurbished, no chain, in probate,* sandblast and crane, high
speed rail link, ice rink, Olympic Park, twin shaft mixers, rotator
wrecker, let a million stray rats and cats out and square meter of
turf where pit-bulls shit and the crack girl knocks and asks
for money to put her electricity back on. Blue boy says *let's build
something here my doll.*

Gully

She's every street ever lived on, sand and dirt and concrete girl. The nightclub magpie hiding in the backstreets watching bricks turn tricks in halflight. She wants to paint the walls green and cover them with palm trees and sail across the Juan de Fuca Straights from Seattle to Vancouver, or sit on the yacht in Crete as the cat sits on her shoulder, whispers *Rat catcher, there is buried treasure inside your baked mud and blubber.* She throws the carpet out of the upstairs window, he doesn't know why she's sleeping on the sofa, why she's checking email on the computer in case there is something else she knows she ought to *watch your back.* Where did she go? To those two lonely willow trees past Stratford station where the God-awful men in shiny suites and the slick oil hair stand around with clip boards counting future's money, and she's all bag of nails and tooth music. She's used and lost it. *rat catcher, bangla tabby, peculiar girl* flies cutty-eyed and foxy, goes back to the heavers, doxy, then she was a kiss-me-kate at the low-tide. *Grow up girl*, big girl, sit in meetings and try talk sense, break from bower and bother, bring a boot-leg plan to a brink, baste yourself in the council office, where you take the bus up the high street and the light railway past the guilt trips and sky scrapes. Grow up tall as Canary Wharf and swim your hand in the river, *shake and shiver girl, cut purse, felon, chor,* they'll CRB you till the cows come home, finger your collar as you look for cubby holes, nooks and hideouts in side streets, *rat-catcher, hi-jacker.* She's only half on the sofa, work late, New Cross Gate, hatched and catch on Haberdashers, the Golden Cross and Kingdom Hall. The shiny teeth and the late night shops, eyes that gleam and gold floss of the chicken bones strewn on cracked roads. It's a small affair. The night caretaker from Lagos calls her a cab, says she's the last one here…

go home green girl, watch your back. Where did she go?

Bright Way.

The house falls down as the site goes up, mixers, fixers and demolition, compulsory purchase orders. Mother Bridget and Papa Ghede meet at the crossroads, *make a wish, cut-glass girl, cutlass girl, cards in your hand.* The River Llew followed a birth canal to a wash up near Three Mills. Hit your ribs at the Karnaphuli, the router's stuck and there's family in India she never knew living on the internet, her baba says, *They're strangers to you, you're made of composite, mass movement and abrasion.* Looks in the mirror to see who she's become. The blue boy makes dolls from drift wood and clay. They turn tricks in the lane next to the theatre. She's a show girl with her feathers, boa and loa, in the Railway Tavern where the workmen drink. *Come in from the cold and have a pint.* They're digging up dirt on the god of light, she googles him in the middle of the night, puts two and two together, Jack be nimble, Jack-be-quick. A phone call, voice, a past of feathers on the roof and, and, and, says his name in the middle of the night. A forgotten spell. Jack jumps over a candlestick.

Go well, go well, cut purse, felon, tricheor.

Hard hat, high viz, work boot, man hole covers, HAZCHEM and exposed cables, caterpillars and crane, nothing to see here. The garden is overgrown, gone and forgotten, a welsh god, a river, a memory of a trip she's taken, a name on the tip of her tongue.

Shambles

She moves her lips from Upton Park to six pound pints in Hackney Wick,
Marie says they'll make money out of the Olympics. The neighbours

she's never met get a petition up to protest about the oldest house
in Stratford's pulled down to make a car park. Angel's caved and gone.

The bhai's in the carpentry shop give her a discount as she's one
of them. The hoods in the black car yell threats to blue boy's eyes,

Don't talk to him like that. What it got to do with you, *sister*, *aunti*,
get yourself an good Indian boy. Mud pools gather in the waste land

near Victory Park. Watch the boom, watch the jib, read the Metro
on the DLR home from Greenwich. *Look sharp girl, fix up, look out girl.*

High Speed girl, jump up and down girl, red door, red light in Maryland
as rain cakes dust and the rat boys ship out to the slums in Leeds. Clean

up the streets, as the sheen of the city boys lick her cheeks.
Look what the cat's dragged in, he batters it with a rolling pin, a
trembling feathered thing.

Rack and Ruts

Separate rooms, her heart in the Mill Stream, his in the ghetto,
her's is *Nellie Dean*, all bright eyes and water floe. She wants
to cross the river and go, he won't go. He won't leave their song
alone, his steel blue eyes whittles sharp, chisels wooden arms,
in his arms where she should be. *She should be his heart's desire,*
Nellie Dean, Nellie Dean. She hears the song in the clang and thump
of the diggers and her broken heart, the foot stamp of boys back
from war, abattoir days where the cattle tread, long gone
with the concert halls. There was an old dive by Pudding Mill where
they murmured about a cut-purse girl, all off her chump and out of pocket.

Flashlock

The reedbeds roll away, break into gravel and grit, a man opens the door of the pub to spit, and it's march home, no home, he says *you can have it all green and dusted*, but it's settled too quick in side her, and flight's cancelled. It's a stew and pickle, they can play in the marsh and churn. Blue boy takes her to the salt water, gives her samphire for tea. She's half there and swallowed as he sucked up the mud.

Street smart girl, cut purse, card sharp, ring-faller, you're mortgaged up in the long game, all up in the East End, everything rains dirt hard and your hidden in the brick dust and can't get out, genie, elf-struck, your peak-a-boo and this isn't Kansas, Tara or a Manhattan night bar. He tries to hold on to what he promised, but she's old mortar, soil grout crumbling and Amerjit hasn't finished the bathroom yet. Marie got upset about so much, took the kids to Ireland, said she'd keep the house in Plaistow as an investment. Hold fast, hand fast, roll the die till the big sleep comes, *one day*, Marie says, *you need to grow up*, tax-break, hippy-shake, grow cold. He tries to hold on to what he promised her, what she vowed, the long game, the long arm of the law. *Are you going to drink all that Absinthe alone?* Safe ways turned to Morrisons and the Flop House's boarded up past Iceland. Chin music and closed head, off the track, pigeon-holed and decked.

Still in that holding cell, reading all the wish-you well graffiti, mug-shot and finger painted, never left the clink, can't escape, no tunnel out until they burrow eight meters underground to Dover. The choke in her lungs thinks it over and over. Chained to the sink.
                                          Think it over, cut price girl.

They redecorate the station, the man in the market says he'll wait for the mushrooms to go off so he can mark them up. *The nobs'll buy*

anything in a brown paper bag if you say it's organic. He winks, like
she knows the blag. The glamour rots inside like a grime tattoo, two
shots of vodka, ice and tequila, buy Absinthe from Safeways,
watch Prime Suspect, avoid big conversations, and when blue boy
gets home, she says *It's over.* He agrees.

Cross Road

She's hobbled, ankles and hip broke, crushed under wrecking and knock
down. Plot dismantled, torn into bits for a dwelling.
Removed restrictions, packs the cat into flat pack and take a hack
to SE23 and contact all the utilities, replaces soak way,

see four paths ahead, stuck in a square of land, next to the nature
reserve, off Forest Hill. Handles the impact, far from the cut off.
Try not to look back, pillars of salt, pinch of salt, take it, *turn again*,
blood's a flag, sniper points into One Tree Hill.

All other sides look at once, desire lines of a cold lung of love, all run
and spilt over the wide Quaker streets, melt straight roads
down, find inroads to charm higardy pigardy, ingots of clay and loam
where Lakshmi turns to Hecate and sits on the oldest tree,

won't come down till she's flinch, sneers and broken vows.
cut purse girl, come with me to the river now
up all night looking for the locket he bought her, lost it, tossed it,
thrown away, turned over and toasted, dip, dyed and hatchet girl.

Grip

Down One Tree Hill to New Cross Gate, SE14, walk to a college
to talk knife crime. The dives are razor sharp and televisions on,
the day is pistol whip and gentleman-of-the-road. She's buffaloed,
clubbed and downed in dodge city tactics, smacked on the left side
of her head, floored outside a New Cross internet café. *You
alright love?* Passers by ask, help her up, *have you had a drink?*
Something hard and fast blows into towers as the smoke knits
and they mumble *shit, pearl harbour* outside the TV shop, walk up
the road, on her own at the apocalypse. Dizzy-head, gun runner,
cut-purse, terrorist.

Cut through

Base girl, top girl, get the bus into Lewisham on time girl. This time, cut purse, toe-rag, sign the rent agreement, no one looks out for you urchin.

cut purse, toe-rag, felon, tramp.

Marie says *hold my hand, life giver, with-woman, be with me,*
take water from the tank and drain me, life bringer, scissor girl,
cut cut Heggidy, giddy girl, bring the boy out. She was stoker, churner,
doubled up and blood-wrecked, pelvis smash and gas and air.
Shit and hair stain and all around is Marie in sweat and drain.
Doubled up, in mucus, puss, dirty juice, and the blood
seeps into a new land lain down in strands on DNA he stares
and thrusts out his arm. His father laughs and calls him Superman.
She holds him up to the Catford Cat, to London, wonder what
he'll be covered in, something for the world made from Marie and Zak,
and Chelsea, Plaistow, Shepherds Bush, Waterford and Azerbaijan,
and they will march to the Embankment, spit in the Thames to stop
the scuds they can't stop, protests with push chairs and baby boom.

Hag-path

A scab forms half way open, artery hurts, pulse cut loose,
time limpits up and spews where she walks, keep walking,
past Essex Road, down Newington Green, into Green Lanes
Church Street, walk carried by force of a half-life, bone-cut,
calcium and ossify, to One Tree Hill, wave to the girl she was
north to south, under mud and rake, *can you hear? Can you
hear across time? Cut-purse, foot-pad, turned into the frog princess
you always were?* Lean against the oldest tree, breathing down
it's spine, it's leaf-litter pour from fingers, fold back into old lanes
and avenues becomes eyes. No more time just a squat of earth
on a railway line.

Frogs

A love can stay in a cooled heart, embers die back as she turns,
writes his name in the mudflats, watches the sink and the basin
erase a man who forgets her, unlearns the colour of her eyes,
neglects her laughter, echo girl, a voice. The city sleeps
and breathes without her, keeps her songs. The story is bigger
then her and flows despite her. She walks away but keeps
some concrete and coal dust, ash from the martyrs inside her guts.
She frees her lungs and cuts ties of lost highways behind her.
Erased on a bypass, a junction and ring road wrapped around
her chest to get lost in, time and time again. The city blooms
so many Narcissus all around her. There must be new frogs and toads
to follow, streets take you where others go, those strange beaten
tracks she can make on her own. She must let the children
she never had go, where she wrote their names on London
roads, the things she stole and never gave back, spells she couldn't
unbind, let them decay. The tongue twisters she told to knot them
together – she can't take them back.

and Toads

She injests the buds and blooms to forget those flower boys, Jack-in the-green, forget-me-not blue, she drives away, into the garden, to the orchards to the deep deep green where she can never be seen, never be sussed, hidden away by the plains of her sights with a *cat on her back, cut purse, felon, Moll.*

Acknowledgements and Thanks

Many Thanks to Aaron Kent and all at Broken Sleep Books for believing in this book. Thanks to the following publishers who have published versions of these poems, *Long Poem Magazine*, *Under the Radar*, *Finished Creatures* and *Molly Bloom*. Skylarker (originally published in Finished Creatures) was highly commended in the 2021 Forward Prize. Thanks to Simon Jones, Jess Whyte and Jemma Borg who read early drafts of Desire Lines. As ever thanks to all my poetry friends and teachers who have supported me through my poetry journey. Thanks to London itself for homing me for 26 years.

Notes on the Language: there are words from the following languages in Desire Lines, notably Romani, Polari, Cant, Rhyming Slang, back slang, Victorian 'Gobbledygook' and other 'anti-languages' and a great book on the subject is Johnathon Green's *Language! 500 Years of the Vulgar Tongue* (Atlantic) 2014.

LAY OUT YOUR UNREST

Ingram Content Group UK Ltd.
Milton Keynes UK
UKHW040830080523
421394UK00003B/85

9 781915 079916